# THE RESPIRATORY SYSTEM

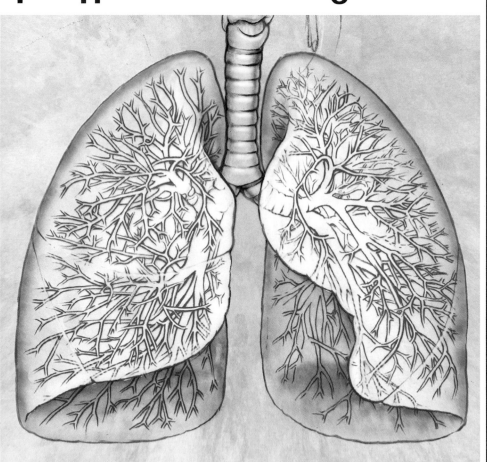

*By Susan H. Gray*

THE CHILD'S WORLD®
CHANHASSEN, MINNESOTA

Published in the United States of America by the Child's World®
P.O. Box 326, Chanhassen, MN 55317-0326
800-599-READ
www.childsworld.com

*Subject adviser:*
*R. John Solaro, Ph.D.,*
*Distinguished*
*University Professor*
*and Head, Department*
*of Physiology and*
*Biophysics, University*
*of Illinois Chicago,*
*Chicago, Illinois*

Photo Credits: Cover: Artville/Scott Bodell; Corbis: 15 (Jean Miele), 18 (Michael Pole), 20 (Lester V. Bergman), 22 (Tom & Dee Ann McCarthy), 23 (LWA-Stephen Welstead), 24 (Ron Boardman; Frank Lane Picture Agency), 26 (Robert Llewellyn); Custom Medical Stock Pictures: 8, 10, 12, 13, 14, 21; PhotoEdit: 5 (Myrleen Ferguson Cate), 6 and 12 (Mary Kate Denny), 7 and 25 (Spencer Grant), 11 (Richard Hutchings), 16 (Alan Oddie), 17 and 27 (Michael Newman).

The Child's World®: Mary Berendes, Publishing Director

Editorial Directions, Inc.: E. Russell Primm, Editorial Director; Elizabeth K. Martin, Line Editor; Katie Marsico, Assistant Editor; Olivia Nellums, Editorial Assistant; Susan Hindman, Copy Editor; Elizabeth K. Martin, Proofreader; Peter Garnham, Marilyn Mallin, Mary Hoffman, Fact Checkers; Tim Griffin/IndexServ, Indexer; Cian Loughlin O'Day, Photo Researcher; Linda S. Koutris, Photo Selector

**Library of Congress Cataloging-in-Publication Data**
Gray, Susan Heinrichs.
 The respiratory system / by Susan H. Gray.
   p. cm. — (Human body)
Contents: What is the respiratory system?—What is the voice box?—Why do you breathe?— What does the blood do?—Some breathing problems. Includes bibliographical references and index.
 ISBN 1-59296-040-5 (Library Bound : alk. paper)
 1. Respiratory organs—Juvenile literature. [1. Respiration. 2. Respiratory system.]
I. Title. II. Series.
 QP121.G674 2003
 612.2—dc21                                                    2003008037

# TABLE OF CONTENTS

# CHAPTER ONE

# Samantha Sings!

It was Samantha's turn to sing. She was not at all excited about this. Getting up in front of everyone made her nervous. But she stood up anyway and nodded to the piano player. The music started, and Samantha took a long, deep breath.

Air rushed into her nose and mouth. It flowed through **passages** in her skull, then down into her throat. Air slipped between flaps of tissue in her throat called vocal cords, then into her chest. It flowed into two tubes—one that leads to the right lung and the other that leads to the left. The air moved deeper and deeper into her lungs. Finally, it could go no farther. It had reached the little air pockets. Millions of the pockets inflated.

Oxygen (OX-ih-jen) in the pockets seeped into the nearby blood vessels. Blood picked up the oxygen and carried it through Samantha's body. Oxygen helped keep all of her tissues working. With oxygen, her leg muscles kept her standing. With oxygen, her brain could think about the music. With oxygen, her ears could hear the piano.

*Samantha's respiratory system helped her whole body prepare to sing.*

*Vocal cords let you sing out loud, as Samantha does, or speak in a tiny whisper.*

Samantha's voice box became tense. Her vocal cords moved close

together. She opened her mouth to sing the first note. Air from her

lungs pushed against the vocal cords. The cords vibrated together, and

the note began to come out. The sound was just beautiful. "Hey, this

isn't so bad," she thought. Samantha's respiratory (RESS-pur-uh-tore-

ee) system was helping her out.

# CHAPTER TWO

# WHAT IS THE RESPIRATORY SYSTEM?

The word *respiratory* comes from a Latin word that means "to breathe." The respiratory system has to do with breathing. It includes more than just the lungs. It involves all of the

*Just breathing in or out puts your respiratory system to work.*

tubes and air **sacs** that fill up and empty as a person breathes. Muscles help expand the lungs and move air in and out of the lungs. Nerves in the brain automatically make the muscles work without you having to think about breathing all the time.

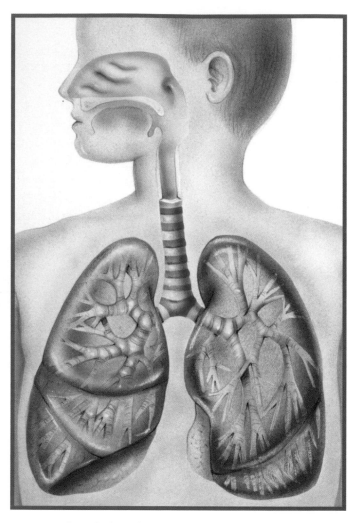

*Air breathed in through the mouth passes through the pharynx and the trachea, moving into the lungs through the bronchi.*

The respiratory system includes the nose, mouth, windpipe, and lungs. Most people do not notice when these organs are working. But each organ plays a big part in breathing.

Each time a person breathes in, or inhales, air passes through the nose or mouth. From there, it moves through the pharynx (FEHR-inx). The pharynx is the area in the upper part of the throat. Air then moves through the voice box and down the windpipe, or trachea (TRAY-kee-uh). This is a tube that is about as wide as a garden hose. In an adult, it is about 4 $^1/2$ inches (10 centimeters) long.

The bottom of the trachea splits into two branches. One branch leads into the right lung. The other leads into the left lung. Each branch is called a bronchus (BRONK-us). The two branches together are called bronchi (BRONK-eye). Each bronchus splits into smaller and smaller branches. The branches become so small that they can barely be seen. At the ends of the tiniest branches are air sacs called alveoli (al-VEE-uh-LIE). One air sac is called an alveolus (al-VEE-uh-luss). The alveoli have moist, thin, delicate walls. Tiny blood vessels wrap around the outside of each alveolus.

The bronchi, their branches, and millions of alveoli make up the lungs. The lungs are in the chest, just behind the ribs. The heart sits right between them. Lungs are very spongy organs. They do not weigh very much. This is because they are full of so many air sacs.

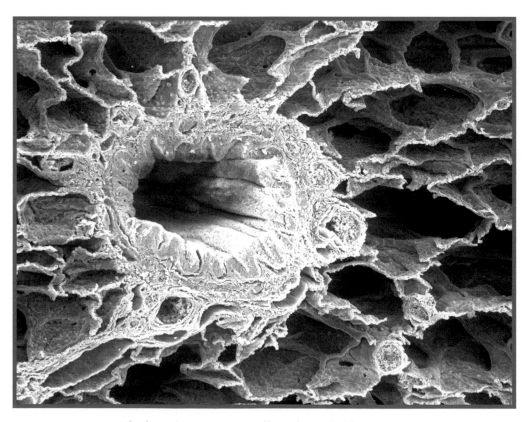

*The bronchi split into smaller tubes called bronchioles.*
*Here is a bronchiole surrounded by many air sacs, or alveoli.*

*When you breath out, your chest and ribs relax, allowing air to move out of the alveoli.*

When a person breathes, some air goes down the left bronchus and some goes down the right one. Air keeps moving through all the branches until it reaches the alveoli. The alveoli fill up with air. The chest and ribs **expand** as this happens. Then the chest and ribs relax. Air moves from the alveoli, back through all the tubes, and out through the mouth or nose.

You can breathe through your mouth or through your nose. Breathing through the mouth might be faster. But breathing through the nose is usually better. This is because the nose does several jobs that the mouth can't. It cleans, warms, and moistens the air.

The nostrils (NOSS-trulz) are the openings of the nose. There are some small hairs in the nostrils. These hairs catch large dirt particles (and sometimes bugs) before they get any farther. The walls inside the nose are lined with cells that make fluid. This fluid keeps the inside of the nose moist. When air comes in, it passes by these moist cells. Dirt and dust from the air get trapped in the fluid. They do not go down into the lungs.

The nose also warms the air passing through it. Air goes up into the nose, through passages in the skull, and down to the pharynx. As it does so, it becomes warm and moist. The lungs work best when they are also warm and moist. So breathing through the nose helps the lungs do their job better.

# CHAPTER THREE

# WHAT IS THE VOICE BOX?

At the top of the trachea is an organ called the voice box, or larynx (LEHR-inx). It is used in speaking, singing, and making other sounds. With each breath, air passes through the larynx, even when no sound is being made.

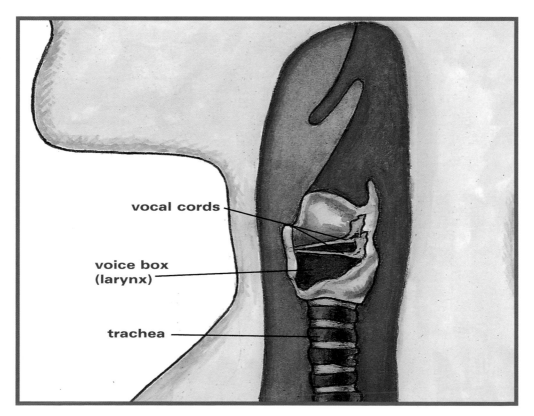

*Air moves through the voice box as you breathe in and out.*

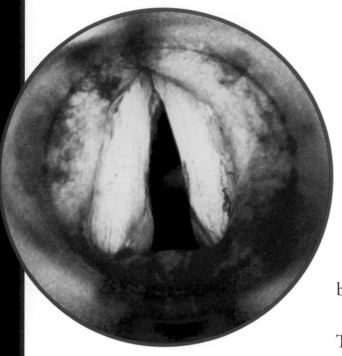
*A doctor's bronchoscope lets us see folds of tissue called the vocal cords.*

Inside the larynx are the vocal cords. They are not really cords at all. They are little folds of soft tissue. One is on the right and one is on the left. When you are breathing, these folds move apart. This allows air to move freely through the voice box.

Usually you inhale before speaking. When you are ready to talk, the folds in the larynx move together. As you exhale, air from your lungs makes the folds vibrate. The vibration makes a sound. You use the roof of your mouth and your lips, tongue, and teeth to turn the sounds into words.

Try speaking while you inhale. You will see this doesn't work so

*Your tongue, lips, and teeth turn the vibrations of the vocal cords into words.*

well. The vocal cords vibrate and make a sound. But it is hard to

breathe in. And some words like "chest" and "sheep" are hard to say.

Air is passing through the mouth in the wrong direction. These words

just cannot be spoken correctly.

# CHAPTER FOUR

# WHY DO YOU BREATHE?

**B**reathing must be very important. After all, you do it all the time, day and night. You breathe for two main reasons. Breathing helps your tissues get the oxygen they need. You also breathe so your tissues can get rid of a waste gas called carbon dioxide (dy-OX-ide).

When you breathe in, your lungs take in air. Air is made up of several different gases. The main gas is nitrogen (NY-truh-jen). Almost four-fifths of the air is made up of this gas. Oxygen makes up about one-

*Even while you are sleeping, your respiratory system is hard at work.*

*The respiratory system brings oxygen to all the parts of your body.*

fifth of the air. The rest of the air is made up of many gases in very

small amounts, including carbon dioxide.

The body's tissues and organs all need oxygen to work properly.

The heart cannot beat without oxygen. The brain cannot think with-

out it. Arm and leg muscles cannot move unless they get oxygen.

*As you go through your day, your body is always using oxygen and producing carbon dioxide.*

As tissues and organs do their work, they create waste materials.

One of these is carbon dioxide. This gas must be removed so tissues

can keep doing their work. The job of the respiratory system is to

bring in oxygen and get rid of the carbon dioxide.

# CHAPTER FIVE

# WHAT DOES THE BLOOD DO?

The respiratory system is in your head, neck, and chest. But what if your toenails need oxygen to grow? How does the oxygen get there? What if your eyelid muscles need to get rid of carbon dioxide? How does that gas get to your lungs?

The lungs do not actually take oxygen to the tissues. And they do not take carbon dioxide away from them. These are jobs for the blood. Special cells in the blood are built just for carrying these gases.

Blood is always on the move. It moves through the tiny vessels next to the alveoli. It moves to the heart. The heart pumps blood out to the body's tissues. It pumps blood down to the toenails and up to the eyelids. It pumps blood all throughout the body. Blood comes back to the heart and is pumped to the lungs. It moves past the alveoli

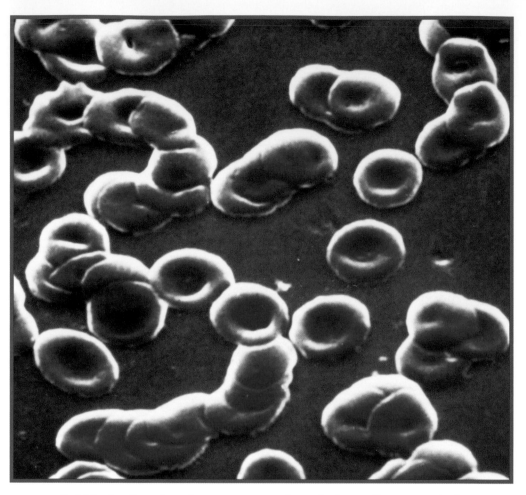

*Red blood cells such as these carry oxygen from the lungs all over your body.*

again. Over and over, all day long, blood makes this trip.

Each time you breathe in, your lungs take in nitrogen, oxygen, and all of those other gases in the air. These gases fill your lungs and inflate the little alveoli. Blood moving alongside the alveoli picks up the oxygen. Loaded with oxygen, blood travels to the heart. The heart pumps it out to the rest of the body. The heart pumps blood to every single tissue and organ. When blood reaches the tissues, oxygen leaves the blood. It goes right into the tissues so they can keep working.

Then carbon dioxide moves from the tissues into the blood. As the blood keeps moving, it hauls the carbon dioxide away. Soon this blood reaches the heart. The heart pumps it right to the lungs. Again,

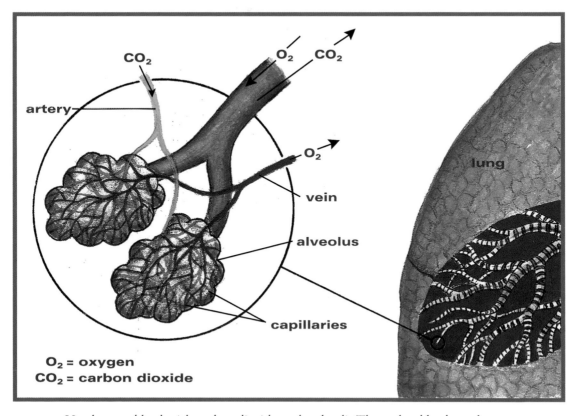

*Vessels carry blood with carbon dioxide to the alveoli. Then other blood vessels carry oxygen-rich blood from the lungs to the heart, then to the rest of the body.*

blood goes into the tiny vessels wrapped around the alveoli. Then carbon dioxide moves out of the blood and into the alveoli. Carbon dioxide leaves the lungs when you breathe out. Then the blood picks up more oxygen and heads back to the heart.

The lungs, heart, and blood all work together. They make sure that every single body part gets oxygen. They see to it that carbon dioxide gets carried away.

*Your heart and blood work with the respiratory system to give your body the oxygen it needs to work.*

Stick your face in a bucket of ice water. Pinch your tongue and pull on it. Eat a lemon. Stand on your head. These are just a few ideas that people have put forth for curing hiccups. Everyone gets hiccups. But what exactly are they?

Hiccups involve the diaphragm (DY-uh-fram). The diaphragm is a large muscle that forms a floor under the lungs. The action of the diaphragm causes you to breathe. When this muscle contracts, it moves down and you inhale. When the diaphragm relaxes, it moves up and you exhale.

Sometimes the diaphragm has spasms (SPAZ-ums). This means it contracts very quickly, over and over. Each time it contracts, you inhale suddenly. Then the vocal cords clap together. They stop air from moving through the voice box. This makes the "hic" sound of hiccups.

Doctors are not exactly sure why people get hiccups. Most people get over them in a few minutes or hours. Sometimes, though, people have them for days. A man from Iowa had the worst case ever known. He had the hiccups for more than 60 years!

# CHAPTER SIX

# SOME BREATHING PROBLEMS

**S**ometimes the respiratory system does not work properly. This is often because the lungs get an infection. Everyone catches the common cold at some time. Colds are caused by about 200 different kinds of viruses. If you have a cold, you often have a sore throat, a cough, and a runny nose. You usually do not have a fever.

A few viruses cause a particular kind of infection. These are the flu viruses. The real name for the flu is

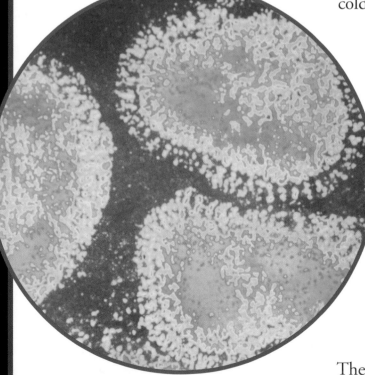

*The flu virus is one of many that can infect your respiratory system.*

*The flu really attacks your respiratory system, but it makes you feel bad all over.*

influenza (IN-flew-EN-zuh). The influenza virus comes in through the

nose or mouth. It attacks the nose, throat, and lungs. A person with

the flu seems to have a cold, but also has a fever.

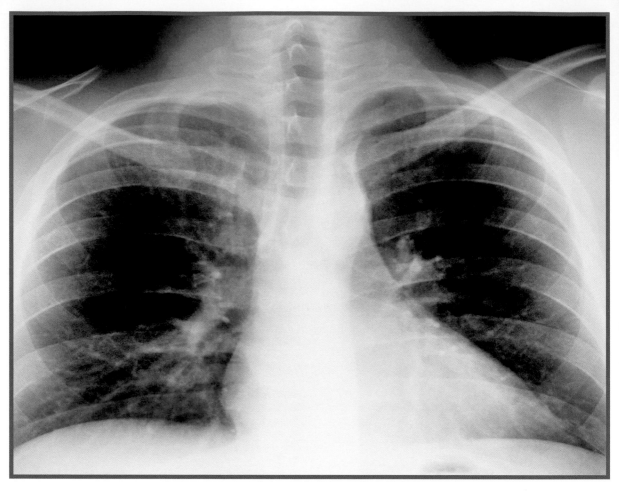

*Smoking clogs people's lungs, making them look black in an X ray. It also makes it very difficult for them to breathe and to go about their normal lives.*

The common cold and the flu are very contagious (kun-TAY-juss) diseases. That means they spread easily from person to person. When an infected person sneezes or coughs, the virus spews out into the air. Someone else breathes it in. Soon, they have the disease, too.

Other things can cause the respiratory system to work poorly.

Smoking is the worst thing for the lungs. Breathing polluted air is also harmful. After years of smoking or breathing dirty air, people can get lung cancer. They feel chest pain and they cough a lot. They also

*Exercising and not smoking will help your respiratory system keep working for years to come.*

feel as though they are not getting enough air.

You can keep your lungs healthy by exercising and by not smoking. A healthy respiratory system can work fine for a lifetime. It cleans the air coming into the body. It draws oxygen into the blood. It gets rid of carbon dioxide. With each breath, it does all of these jobs. And every day, it takes more than 20,000 breaths. The respiratory system never rests. It does an incredible job.

# Glossary

**cells (selz)** Cells are the small units in a living organism. In humans, cells make up tissues.

**contracts (kuhn-TRAKTZ)** To contract is to squeeze up or shorten.

**expand (ek-SPAND)** To expand is to get bigger or to enlarge.

**passages (PASS-ih-jez)** Passages are pathways.

**sacs (SAKS)** A sac is a part that is shaped like a little bag or pocket.

# Questions and Answers about the Respiratory System

**What is asthma?** Asthma is a lung condition common in children. It is caused when the lungs are overly sensitive to dust, smoke, and other things in the air, or to exercise. The airways react to these things by closing up, making it very difficult to breathe.

**Why are cigarettes bad for my lungs?** When you smoke a cigarette, you are letting many chemicals into your lungs. These chemicals mix together to form tar, which sticks to your lungs. It prevents your lungs from keeping out germs and dirt that cause diseases of your respiratory system.

**Why do people snore?** Vibrating tissues in your air passages make those funny snoring sounds. Snoring can be caused by many different things. Having a stuffy nose or being overweight can make you snore. So can sleep apnea, a condition in which you stop breathing while you sleep. If tissues in your nose are too large, they might make you snore, too. Sometimes sleeping on your side instead of on your back can help prevent snoring.

# Did You Know?

- The left lung is a little smaller than the right lung. This is because the bottom of the heart tilts a little to the left. It takes away some space from the left lung.

- The average person has more than 600 million alveoli.

- Some people have a big Adam's apple. This is a bump that often sticks out in the front of the neck. The Adam's apple is really a part of the voice box.

- Certain seals can hold their breath for more than an hour underwater. During this time, they use oxygen that is already stored in their tissues.

- Some people have a problem called sleep apnea (AP-nee-uh). As they sleep, they often stop breathing, sometimes for 30 seconds or longer.

# How to Learn More about the Respiratory System

## At the Library

Hayhurst, Chris.
*The Lungs: Learning How We Breathe.*
New York: Rosen Publishing Group, 2002.

Lambert, Mark.
*The Lungs and Breathing.*
Englewood Cliffs, N.J.: Silver Burdett Press, 1988.

Parker, Steve.
*The Lungs and Respiratory System.*
Austin, Tex.: Raintree/Steck-Vaughn, 1997.

## On the Web

Visit our home page for lots of links about the respiratory system:
*http://www.childsworld.com/links.html*
Note to Parents, Teachers, and Librarians: We routinely verify our
Web links to make sure they're safe, active sites—so encourage
your readers to check them out!

## Through the Mail or by Phone

THE AMERICAN LUNG ASSOCIATION
61 Broadway, 6th Floor
NY, NY 10006
212-315-8700
*http://www.lungusa.org*

NATIONAL HEART, LUNG, AND BLOOD INSTITUTE
NHLBI Health Information Center
Attention: Web Site
P.O. Box 30105
Bethesda, MD 20824-0105
301-592-8573
*http://www.nhlbi.nih.gov*

NATIONAL INSTITUTE OF ALLERGY AND INFECTIOUS DISEASES
Building 31, Room 7A-50
31 Center Drive MSC 2520
Bethesda, MD 20892-2520
*http://www.niaid.nih.gov*

# Index

## About the Author

**Susan H. Gray** has a bachelor's and a master's degree in zoology, and has taught college-level anatomy and physiology courses. In her 25 years as an author, she has written many medical articles, grant proposals, and children's books. Ms. Gray enjoys gardening, traveling, and playing the piano and organ. She has traveled twice to the Russian Far East to give organ workshops to church musicians. She also works extensively with American and Russian friends to develop medical and social service programs for Vladivostok, Russia. Ms. Gray and her husband, Michael, live in Cabot, Arkansas.